Love and Self Love

Louisa May Alcott

Table of Contents

Love and Self Love

Louisa May Alcott

FRIENDLESS, when you are gone? But, Jean, you surely do not mean that Effie has no claim on any human creature, beyond the universal one of common charity ?" I said, as she ceased, and lay panting on her pillows, with her sunken eyes fixed eagerly upon my own.

"Ay, Sir, I do; for her grandfather has never by word or deed acknowledged her, or paid the least heed to the letter her poor mother sent him from her dying bed seven years ago. He is a lone old man, and this child is the last of his name; yet he will not see her, and cares little whether she be dead or living. It's a bitter shame, Sir, and the memory of it will rise up before him when he comes to lie where I am lying now."

"And you have kept the girl safe in the shelter of your honest home all these years? Heaven will remember that, and in the great record of good deeds will set the name of Adam Lyndsay far below that of poor Jean Burns," I said, pressing the thin hand that had succored the orphan in her need.

But Jean took no honor to herself for that charity, and answered simply to my words of commendation.

"Sir, her mother was my foster–child; and when she left that stern old man for love of Walter Home, I went, too, for love of her. Ah, dear heart! she had sore need of me in the

1

weary wanderings which ended only when she lay down by her dead husband's side and left her bairn to me. Then I came here to cherish her among kind souls where I was born; and here she has grown up, an innocent young thing safe from the wicked world, the comfort of my life, and the one thing I grieve at leaving when the time that is drawing very near shall come."

"Would not an appeal to Mr. Lyndsay reach him now, think you? Might not Effie go to him herself ? Surely, the sight of such a winsome creature would touch his heart, however hard."

But Jean rose up in her bed, crying, almost fiercely,—

"No, Sir! no! My child shall never go to beg a shelter in that hard man's house. I know too well the cold looks, the cruel words, that would sting her high spirit and try her heart, as they did her mother's. No, Sir,—rather than that, she shall go with Lady Gower."

"Lady Gower ? What has she to do with Effie, Jean?" I asked, with increasing interest.

"She will take Effie as her maid, Sir. A hard life for my child! but what can I do?" And Jean's keen glance seemed trying to read mine.

"A waiting–maid? Heaven forbid!" I ejaculated, as a vision of that haughty lady and her three wild sons swept through my mind.

I rose, paced the room in silence for a little time, then took a sudden resolution, and, turning to the bed, exclaimed,—

"Jean, I will adopt Effie. I am old enough to be her father; and she shall never feel the want of one, if you will give her to my care."

To my surprise, Jean's eager face wore a look of disappointment as she listened, and with a sigh replied,—

"That's a kind thought, Sir, and a generous one; but it cannot be as you wish. You may be twice her age, but still too young for that. How could Effie look into that face of yours, so bonnie, Sir, for all it is so grave, and, seeing never a wrinkle on the forehead, nor a white

2

hair among the black, how could she call you father? No, it will not do, though so kindly meant. Your friends would laugh at you, Sir, and idle tongues might speak ill of my bairn."

"Then what can I do, Jean?" I asked, regretfully.

"Make her your wife, Sir."

I turned sharply and stared at the woman, as her abrupt reply reached my ear.

Though trembling for the consequence of her boldly spoken wish, Jean did not shrink from my astonished gaze; and when I saw the wistfulness of that wan face, the smile died on my lips, checked by the tender courage which had prompted the utterance of her dying hope.

"My good Jean, you forget that Effie is a child, and I a moody, solitary man, with no gifts to win a wife or make home happy."

"Effie is sixteen, Sir,—a fair, good lassie for her years; and you—ah, Sir, you may call yourself unfit for wife and home, but the poorest, saddest creature in this place knows that the man whose hand is always open, whose heart is always pitiful, is not the one to live alone, but to win and to deserve a happy home and a true wife. Oh, Sir, forgive me, if I leave been too bold; but my time is short, and I love my child so well, I cannot leave the desire of my heart unspoken, for it is my last."

As the words fell brokenly from her lips, and tears streamed down her pallid cheek, a great pity took possession of me, the old longing to find some solace for my solitary life returned again, and peace seemed to smile on me from little Effie's eyes.

"Jean," I said, "give me till to—morrow to consider this new thought. I fear it cannot be; but I have learned to love the child too well to see her thrust out from the shelter of your home to walk through this evil world alone. I will consider your proposal, and endeavor to devise some future for the child which shall set your heart at rest. But before you urge this further, let me tell you that I am not what you think me. I am a cold, selfish man, often gloomy, often stern,—a most unfit guardian for a tender creature like this little girl. The deeds of mine which you call kind are not true charities; it frets me to see pain, and I

3

desire my ease above all earthly things. You are grateful for the little I have done for you, and deceive yourself regarding my true worth; but of one thing you may rest assured,—I am an honest man, who holds his name too high to stain it with a false word or a dishonorable deed."

"I do believe you, Sir," Jean answered, eagerly. "And if I left the child to you, I could die this night in peace. Indeed, Sir, I never should have dared to speak of this, but for the belief that you loved the girl. What else could I think, when you came so often and were so kind to us ? "

"I cannot blame you, Jean; it was my usual forgetfulness of others which so misled you. I was tired of the world, and came hither to find peace in solitude. Effie cheered me with her winsome ways, and I learned to look on her as the blithe spirit whose artless wiles won me to forget a bitter past and a regretful present." I paused; and then added, with a smile, "But, in our wise schemes, we have overlooked one point: Effie does not love me, and may decline the future you desire me to offer her."

A vivid hope lit those dim eyes, as Jean met my smile with one far brighter, and joyfully replied,—

"She does love you, Sir; for you have given her the greatest happiness she has ever known. Last night she sat looking silently into the fire there with a strange gloom on her bonnie face, and, when I asked what she was dreaming of, she turned to me with a look of pain and fear, as if dismayed at some great loss, but she only said, 'He is going Jean! What shall I do ?'"

"Poor child! she will miss her friend and teacher, when I'm gone; and I shall miss the only human creature that has seemed to care for me for years," I sighed,— adding, as I paused upon the threshold of the door, "Say nothing of this to Effie till I come to–morrow, Jean."

I went away, and far out on the lonely moor sat down to think. Like a weird magician, Memory led me back into the past, calling up the hopes and passions buried there. My childhood,— fatherless and motherless, but not unhappy; for no wish was ungratified, no idle whim denied. My boyhood,— with no shadows over it but those my own wayward will called up. My manhood,— when the great joy of my life arose, my love for Agnes, a

Love and Self Love

midsummer dream of bloom and bliss, so short–lived and so sweet! I felt again the pang that wrung my heart when she coldly gave me back the pledge I thought so sacred and so sure, and the music of her marriage bells tolled the knell of my lost love. I seemed to hear them still wafted across the purple moor through the silence of those fifteen years.

My life looked gray and joyless as the wide waste lying hushed around me, unblessed with the verdure of a single hope, a single love; and as I looked down the coming years, my way seemed very solitary, very dark.

Suddenly a lark soared upward from the heath, cleaving the silence with its jubilant song. The sleeping echoes woke, the dun moor seemed to smile, and the blithe music fell like dew upon my gloomy spirit, wakening a new desire.

What this bird is to the moor might little Effie be to me," I thought within myself, longing to possess the cheerful spirit which had power to gladden me.

"Yes," I mused, "The old home will seem more solitary now than ever; and if I cannot win the lark's song without a golden fetter, I will give it one, and while it sings for love of me it shall not know a want or fear."

Heaven help me! I forgot the poor return I made my lark for the sweet liberty it lost.

All that night I pondered the altered future Jean had laid before me, and the longer I looked the fairer it seemed to grow. Wealth I cared nothing for; the world's opinion I defied; ambition had departed, and passion I believed lay dead;— then why should I deny myself the consolation which seemed offered to me? I would accept it; and as I resolved, the dawn looked in at me, fresh and fair as little Effie's face.

I met Jean with a smile, and, as she read its significance aright, there shone a sudden peace upon her countenance, more touching than her grateful words.

Effie came singing from the burn–side, as unconscious of the change which awaited her as the flowers gathered in her plaid and crowning her bright hair.

I drew her to my side, and in the simplest words asked her if she would go with me when Jean's long guardianship was ended. Joy, sorrow, and surprise stirred the sweet composure of her face, and quickened the tranquil beating of her heart. But as I ceased, joy conquered grief and wonder; for she clapped her hands like a glad child, exclaiming,—

"Go with you, Sir ? Oh, if you knew how I long to see the home you have so often pictured to me, you would never doubt my willingness to go."

"But, Effie, you do not understand. Are you willing to go with me as my wife?" I said,— with a secret sense of something like remorse, as I uttered that word, which once meant so much to me, and now seemed such an empty title to bestow on her.

The flowers dropped from the loosened plaid, as Effie looked with a startled glance into my face; the color left her cheeks, and the smile died on her lips, but a timid joy lit her eye, as she softly echoed my last words,—

"Your wife? It sounds very solemn though so sweet. Ah, Sir, I am not wise or good enough for that !"

A child's humility breathed in her speech, but something of a woman's fervor shone in her uplifted countenance, and sounded in the sudden tremor of her voice.

Effie, I want you as you are," I said,— "no wiser, dear,— no better. I want your innocent affection to appease the hunger of an empty heart, your blithe companionship to cheer my solitary home. Be still a child to me, and let me give you the protection of my name."

Effie turned to her old friend, and, laying her young face on the pillow close beside the worn one grown so dear to her, asked, in a tone half pleading, half regretful,—

"Dear Jean, shall I go so far away from you and the home you gave me when I had no other? "

"My bairn, I shall not be here, and it will never seem like home with old Jean gone. It is the last wish I shall ever know, to see you safe with this good gentleman who loves my child. Go, dear heart, and be happy; and heaven bless and keep you both!"

Love and Self Love

Jean held her fast a moment, and then, with a whispered prayer, put her gently away. Effie came to me, saying, with a look more eloquent than her meek words,—

"Sir, I will be your wife, and love you very truly all my life."

I drew the little creature to my breast, and felt a tender pride in knowing she was mine. Something in the shy caress those soft arms gave touched my cold nature with a generous warmth, and the innocence of that confiding heart was an appeal to all that made my manhood worth possessing.

Swiftly those few weeks passed, and when old Jean was laid to her last sleep, little Effie wept her grief away upon her husband's bosom, and soon learned to smile in her new English home. Its gloom departed when she came, and for a while it was a very happy place. My bitter moods seemed banished by the magic of the gentle presence that made sunshine there, and I was conscious of a fresh grace added to the life so wearisome before.

I should have been a father to the child, watchful, wise, and tender; but old Jean was right,— I was too young to feel a father's calm affection or to know a father's patient care. I should have been her teacher, striving to cultivate the nature given to my care, and fit it for the trials Heaven sends to all. I should have been a friend, if nothing more, and given her those innocent delights that make youth beautiful and its memory sweet.

I was a master, content to give little, while receiving all she could bestow.

Forgetting her loneliness, I fell back into my old way of life. I shunned the world, because its gayeties had lost their zest. I did not care to travel, for home now possessed a charm it never had before. I knew there was an eager face that always brightened when I came, little feet that flew to welcome me, and hands that loved to minister to every want of mine. Even when I sat engrossed among my books, there was a pleasant consciousness that I was the possessor of a household sprite whom a look could summon and a gesture banish. I loved her as I loved a picture or a flower,— a little better than my horse and hound,— but far less than I loved my most unworthy self.

And she,— always so blithe when I was by, so diligent in studying my desires, so full of simple arts to will my love and prove her gratitude,— she never asked for any boon, and

7

seemed content to live alone with me in that still place, so utterly unlike the home she had left. I had not learned to read that true heart then. I saw those happy eyes grow wistful when I went, leaving her alone; I missed the roses from her cheek, faded for want of gentler care; and when the buoyant spirit which had been her chiefest charm departed, I fancied, in my blindness, that she pined for the free air of the Highlands, and tried to win it back by transient tenderness and costly gifts. But I had robbed my lark of heaven's sunshine, and it could not sing.

I met Agnes again. She was a widow, and to my eye seemed fairer than when I saw her last, and far more kind. Some soft regret seemed shining on me from those lustrous eyes, as if she hoped to win my pardon for that early wrong. I never could forget the deed that darkened my best years, but the old charm stole over me at times, and, turning from the meek child at my feet, I owned the power of the stately woman whose smile seemed a command.

I meant no wrong to Effie, but, looking on her as a child, I forgot the higher claim I had given her as a wife, and, walking blindly on my selfish way, I crushed the little flower I should have cherished in my breast.

"Effie, my old friend Agnes Vaughan is coming, here to–day; so make yourself fair, that you may do honor to my choice; for she desires to see you, and I wish my Scotch harebell to look lovely to this English rose," I said, half playfully, half earnestly, as we stood together looking out across the flowery lawn, one summer day.

"Do you like me to be pretty, Sir?" she answered, with a flush of pleasure on her upturned face. "I will try to make myself fair with the gifts you are always heaping on me; but even then I fear I shall not do you honors nor please your friend, I am so small and young."

A careless reply was on my lips, but, seeing what a long way down the little figure was, I drew it nearer, saying, with a smile, which I knew would make an answering one,—

"Dear, there must lie the bud before the flower; so never grieve, for your youth keeps my spirit young. To me you may be a child forever; but you must learn to be a stately little Madam Ventnor to my friends."

Love and Self Love

She laughed a gayer laugh than I had heard for many a day, and soon departed, intent on keeping well the promise she had given. An hour later, as I sat busied among my books, a little figure glided in, and stood before me with its jewelled arms demurely folded on its breast. It was Effie, as I had never see her before. Some new freak possessed her, for with her girlish dress she seemed to have laid her girlhood by. The brown locks were gathered up, wreathing, the small head like a coronet; aerial lace and silken vesture shimmered in the light and became her well. She looked and moved a fairy queen, stately and small.

I watched her in a silent maze, for the face with its shy blushes and downcast eyes did not seem the childish one turned frankly to my own an hour ago. With a sigh I looked up at Agnes's picture, the sole ornament of that room, and when I withdrew my gaze the blooming vision had departed. I should have followed it to make my peace, but I fell into a fit of bitter musing, and forgot it till Agnes's voice sounded at my door.

She came with a brother, and seemed eager to see my young wife; but Effie did not appear, and I excused her absence as a girlish freak, smiling at it with them, while I chafed inwardly at her neglect, forgetting that I might have been the cause.

Pacing down the garden paths with Agnes at my side, our steps were arrested by a sudden sight of Effie fast asleep among the flowers. She looked a flower herself, lying with her flushed cheek pillowed on her arm, sunshine glittering on the ripples of her hair, and the changeful lustre of her dainty dress. Tears moistened her long lashes, but her lips smiled as if in the blissful land of dreams she had found some solace for her grief.

"A 'Sleeping Beauty' worthy the awakening of any prince!" whispered Alfred Vaughan, pausing with admiring eyes.

A slight frown swept over Agnes's face, but vanished as she said, with that low toned laugh that never seemed unmusical before,— "We must pardon Mrs. Ventnor's seeming rudeness, if she welcomes us with graceful scenes like this. A child–wife's whims are often prettier than the world's formal ways; so do not chide her, Basil, when she wakes."

I was a proud man then, touched easily by trivial things. Agnes's pitying manner stung me, and the tone in which I wakened Effie was far harsher than it should have been. She sprang up; and with a gentle dignity most new to me received her guests, and played the part of hostess with a grace that well atoned for her offence.

Love and Self Love

Agnes watched her silently as she went before us with young Vaughan, and even I, ruffled as my temper was, felt a certain pride in the loving creature who for my sake conquered her timidity and strove to do me honor. But neither by look nor word did I show my satisfaction, for Agnes demanded the constant service of lips and eyes, and I was only too ready to devote them to the woman who still felt her power and dared to show it.

All that day I was beside her, forgetful in many ways of the gentle courtesies I owed the child whom I had made my wife. I did not see the wrong then, but others did, and the deference I failed to show she could ask of them.

In the evening, as I stood near Agnes while she sang the songs we both remembered well, my eye fell on a mirror that confronted me, and in it I saw Effie bending forward with a look that startled me. Some strong emotion controlled her, for with lips apart and eager eyes she gazed keenly at the countenances she believed unconscious of her scrutiny.

Agnes caught the vision that had arrested the half–uttered compliment upon my lips, and, turning, looked at Effie with a smile just touched with scorn.

The color rose vividly to Effie's cheek, but her eyes did not fall,— they sought my face, and rested there. A half–smile crossed my lips; with a sudden impulse I beckoned, and she came with such an altered countenance I fancied that I had not seen aright.

At my desire she sang the ballads she so loved, and in her girlish voice there was an undertone of deeper melody than when I heard them first among her native hills; for the child's heart was ripening fast into the woman's.

Agnes went, at length, and I heard Effie's sigh of relief when we were left alone, but only bid her "go and rest," while I paced to and fro, still murmuring the refrain of Agnes's song.

The Vaughans came often, and we went often to them in the summer–home they had chosen near us on the river–bank. I followed my own wayward will, and Effie's wistful eyes grew sadder as the weeks went by.

Love and Self Love

One sultry evening as we strolled together on the balcony, I was seized with a sudden longing to hear Agnes sing, and bid Effie come with me for a moonlight voyage down the river.

She had been very silent all the evening, with a pensive shadow on her face and rare smiles on her lips. But as I spoke, she paused abruptly, and, clenched her small hands, turned upon me with defiant eyes,— crying, almost fiercely.—

"No, I will not go to listen to that woman's songs. I hate her! yes, more than I can tell! for, till she came, I thought you loved me; but now you think of her alone, and chide me when I look unhappy. You treat me like a child; but I am not one. Oh, Sir, be more kind, for I have only you to love!"— and as her voice died in that sad appeal, she clasped her hands before her face with such a burst of tears that I had no words to answer her.

Disturbed by the sudden passion of the hitherto meek girl, I sat down on the wide steps of the balcony and essayed to draw her to my knee, hoping she would weep this grief away as she had often done a lesser sorrow. But she resisted my caress, and, standing erect before me, checked her tears, saying in a voice still trembling with resentment and reproach,—

"You promised Jean to be kind to me, and you are cruel; for when I ask for love, you give me jewels, books, or flowers, as you would give a pettish child a toy, and go away as if you were weary of me. Oh, it is not right, Sir! and I cannot, no, I will not bear it!"

If she had spared reproaches, deserved though they were, and humbly pleaded to be loved, I should have been more just and gentle; but her indignant words, the sharper for their truths, roused the despotic spirit of the man, and made me sternest when I should have been most kind.

"Effie," I said, looking coldly up into her troubled face, "I have given you the right to be thus frank with me; but before you exercise that right, let me tell you what may silence your reproaches and teach you to know me better. I desired to adopt you as my child; Jean would not consent to that, but bid me marry you, and so give you a home, and win for myself a companion who should make that home less solitary. I could protect you in no other way, and I married you. I meant it kindly, Effie; for I pitied you,— ay, and loved you, too, as I hoped I had fully proved."

11

Love and Self Love

"You have, Sir,— oh, you have! But I hoped I might in time be more to you than a dear child," sighed Effie, while softer tears flowed as she spoke.

"Effie, I told Jean I was a hard, cold man,"— and I was one as those words passed my lips. "I told her I was unfitted to make a wife happy. But she said you would be content with what I could offer; and so I gave you all I had to bestow. It was not enough; yet I cannot make it more. Forgive me, child, and try to bear your disappointments as I have learned to bear mine."

Effie bent suddenly, saying, with a look of anguish, "Do you regret that I am your wife, Sir?"

"Heaven knows I do, for I cannot make you happy," I answered, mournfully.

"Let me go away where I can never grieve or trouble you again! I will,—indeed, I will,— for anything is easier to bear than this. Oh, Jean, why did you leave me when you went?"—and with that despairing cry Effie stretched her arms into the empty air, as if seeking that lost friend.

My anger melted, and I tried to soothe her, saying gently, as I laid her tear–wet cheek to mine,—

"My child, death alone must part us two. We will be patient with each other, and so may learn to be happy yet."

A long silence fell upon us both. My thoughts were busy with the thought of what a different home mine might have been, if Agnes had been true; and Effie— God only knows how sharp a conflict passed in that young heart! I could not guess it till the bitter sequel of that hour came.

A timid hand upon my own aroused me, and, looking down, I met such an altered face, it touched me like a mute reproach. All the passion had died out, and a great patience seemed to have arisen there. It looked so meek and wan, I bent and kissed it; but no smile answered me as Effie humbly said,—

Love and Self Love

"Forgive me, Sir, and tell me how I can make you happier. For I am truly grateful for all you have done for me, and will try to be a docile child to you."

"Be happy yourself, Effie, and I shall be content. I am too grave and old to be a fit companion for you, dear. You shall have gay faces and young friends to make this quiet place more cheerful. I should have thought of that before. Dance, sing, be merry, Effie, and never let your life be darkened by Basil Ventnor's changeful moods."

"And you?" she whispered, looking up.

"I will sit among my books, or seek alone the few friends I care to see, and never mar your gayety with my gloomy presence, dear. We must begin at once to go our separate ways; for, with so many years between us, we can never find the same paths pleasant very long. Let me be a father to you, and a friend,— I cannot be a lover, child."

Effie rose and went silently away; but soon came again, wrapped in her n mantle, saying, as she looked down at me, with something of her former cheerfulness,—

"I am good now. Come and row me down the river. It is too beautiful a night to be spent in tears and naughtiness."

"No, Effie, you shall never go to Mrs. Vaughan's again, if you dislike her so. No friendship of mine need be shared by you, if it gives you pain."

"Nothing shall pain me any more," she answered, with a patient sigh. "I will be your merry girl again, and try to love Agnes for your sake. Ah! do come; father, or I shall not feel forgiven."

Smiling at her April moods, I obeyed the small hands clasped about my own and through the fragrant linden walk went musing to the river–side.

Silently we floated down, and at the lower landing–place found Alfred Vaughan just mooring his own boat. By him I sent a message to his sister, while we waited for her at the shore.

Love and Self Love

Effie stood above me on the sloping bank, and as Agnes entered the green vista of the flowery path, she turned and clung to me with sudden fervor, kissed me passionately, and then stole silently into the boat.

he moonlight turned the waves to silver, and in its magic rays the face of my first love grew young again. She sat before me with water–lilies in her shining hair, singing as she sang of old, while the dub of falling oars kept time to her low song. As we neared the ruined bridge, whose single arch still cast its heavy shadow far across the stream, Agnes bent toward me, softly saying,—

" Basil, you remember this ? "

How could I forget that happy night, long years ago, when she and I went floating down the same bright stream, two happy lovers just betrothed? As she spoke, it all came back more beautiful than ever, and I forgot the silent figure sitting there behind me. I hope Agnes had forgotten, too; for, cruel as she was to me, I never wished to think her hard enough to hate that gentle child.

"I remember, Agnes," I said, with a regretful sigh." My voyage has been a lonely one since then."

"Are you not happy, Basil?" she asked, with a tender pity thrilling her low voice.

"Happy?" I echoed, bitterly,— "how can I be happy, remembering what might have been?"

Agnes bowed her head upon her hands, and silently the boat shot into the black shadow of the arch. A sudden eddy seemed to sway us slightly from our course, and the waves dashed sullenly against the gloomy walls; a moment more and we glided into calmer waters and unbroken light. I looked up from my task to speak, but the words were frozen on my lips by a cry from Agnes, who, wild–eyed and pale, seemed pointing to some phantom which I could not see. I turned,— the phantom was Effie's empty seat. The shining stream grew dark before me, and a great pang of remorse wrung my heart as that sight met my eyes.

Love and Self Love

"Effie!" I cried, with a cry that rent the stillness of the night, and sent the name ringing down the river. But nothing answered me, and the waves rippled softly as they hurried by. Far over the wide stream went my despairing glance, and saw nothing but the lilies swaying as they slept, and the black arch where my child went down.

Agnes lay trembling at my feet, but I never heeded her,— for Jean's dead voice sounded in my ear, demanding the life confided to my care. I listened, benumbed with guilty fear, and, as if summoned by that weird cry, there came a white flash through the waves, and Effie's face rose up before me.

Pallid and wild with the agony of that swift plunge, it confronted me. No cry for help parted the pale lips, but those wide eyes were luminous with a love whose fire that deathful river could not quench.

Like one in an awful dream, I gazed till the ripples closed above it. One instant the terror held me,— the next I was far down in those waves, so silver fair above, so black and terrible below. A brief, blind struggle passed before I grasped a tress of that long hair, then an arm, and then the white shape, with a clutch like death. As the dividing waters gave us to the light again, Agnes hung herself far over the boatside and drew my lifeless burden in; I followed, and we laid it down, a piteous sight for human eyes to look upon. Of that swift voyage home I can remember nothing but the still face on Agnes's breast, the sight of which nerved my dizzy brain and made my muscles iron.

For many weeks there was a darkened chamber in my house, and anxious figures gliding to and fro, wan with long vigils and the fear of death. I often crept in to look upon the little figure lying there, to watch the feverish roses blooming on the wasted cheek, the fitful fire burning in the unconscious eye, to hear the broken words so full of pathos to my ear, and then to steal away and struggle to forget.

My bird fluttered on the threshold of its cage, but Love lured it back, for its gentle mission was not yet fulfilled.

The child Effie lay dead beneath the ripples of the river, but the woman rose up from that bell of suffering like one consecrated to life's high duties by the bitter baptism of that dark hour.

Love and Self Love

Slender and pale, with serious eyes and quiet steps, she moved through the home which once echoed to the glad voice and dancing feet of that vanished shape. A sweet sobriety shaded her young face, and a meek smile sat upon her lips, but the old blithesomeness was gone.

She never claimed her childish place upon my knee, never tried the winsome wiles that used to chase away my gloom, never came to pour her innocent delight and griefs into my ear, or bless me with the frank affection which grew very precious when I found it lost.

Docile as ever, and eager to gratify my lightest wish, she left no wifely duty unfulfilled. Always near me, if I breathed her name, but vanishing when I grew silent, as if her task were done. Always smiling a cheerful farewell when I went, a quiet welcome when I came. I missed the April face that once watched me go, the warm embrace that greeted me again, and at my heart the sense of loss grew daily deeper as I felt the growing change.

Effie remembered the words I had spoken on that mournful night; remembered that our paths must lie apart,— that her husband was a friend, and nothing more. She treasured every careless hint I had given, and followed it most faithfully. She gathered gay, young friends about her, went out into the brilliant world, and I believed she was content.

If I had ever felt she was a burden to the selfish freedom I desired, I was punished now, for I had lost a blessing which no common pleasure could replace. I sat alone, and no blithe voice made music in the silence of my room, no bright locks swept my shoulder, and no soft caress assured me that I was beloved.

I looked for my household sprite in girlish garb, with its free hair and sunny eyes, but found only a fair woman, graceful in rich attire, crowned with my gifts, and standing afar off among her blooming peers. I could not guess the solitude of that true heart, nor see the captive spirit gazing at me from those steadfast eyes.

No word of the cause of that despairing deed passed Effie's lips, and I had no need to ask it. Agnes was silent, and soon left us, but her brother was a frequent guest. Effie liked his gay companionship, and I denied her nothing,— nothing but the one desire of her life.

16

Love and Self Love

So that first year passed; and though the ease and liberty I coveted were undisturbed, I was not satisfied. Solitude grew irksome, and study ceased to charm. I tried old pleasures, but they had lost their zest,— renewed old friendships, but they wearied me. I forgot Agnes, and ceased to think her fair. I looked at Effie, and sighed for my lost youth.

My little wife grew very beautiful, to me, for she was blooming fast into a gracious womanhood. I felt a secret pride in knowing she was mine, and watched her as I fancied a fond brother might, glad that she vas so good, so fair, so much beloved. I ceased to mourn the plaything I had lost, and something akin to reverence mingled with the deepening admiration of the man.

Gay guests had filled the house with festal light and sound one winter's night, and when the last bright figure had vanished from the threshold of the door, I still stood there, looking over the snow–shrouded lawn, hoping to cool the fever of my blood, and ease the restless pain that haunted me.

I shut out the keen air and wintry sky, at length, and silently ascended to the deserted rooms above. But in the gloom of a vestibule my steps were stayed. Two figures, in a flowery alcove, fixed my eye. The light streamed full upon them, and the fragrant stillness of the air was hardly stirred by their low tones.

Effie was there, sunk on a low couch her face bowed upon her hands; and a her side, speaking with impassioned voice and ardent eyes, leaned Alfred Vaughan.

The sight struck me like a blow, and the sharp anguish of that moment proved how deeply I had learned to love.

"Effie, it is a sinful tie that binds you to that man; he does not love you, and it should be broken,— for this slavery will wear away the life now grown so dear to me."

The words, hot with indignant passion, smote me like a wintry blast, but not so coolly as the broken voice that answered them:—

"He said death alone must part us two, and, remembering that, I cannot listen to another love."

Love and Self Love

Like a guilty ghost I stole away, and in the darkness of my solitary room struggled with my bitter grief, my newborn love. I never blamed my wife,— that wife who had heard the tender name so seldom, she could scarce feel it hers. I had fettered her free heart, forgetting it would one day cease to be a child's. I bade her look upon me as a father; she had learned the lesson well; and now what right had I to reproach her for listening to a lover's voice, when her husband's was so cold ? What mattered it that slowly, almost unconsciously, I had learned to love her with the passion of a youth, the power of a man ? I had alienated that fond nature from my own, and now it was too late.

Heaven only knows the bitterness of that hour;— I cannot tell it. But through the darkness of my anguish and remorse that newly kindled love burned like a blessed fire, and, while it tortured, purified. By its light I saw the error of my life: self−love was written on the actions of the past, and I knew that my punishment was very just. With a child's repentant tears, I confessed it to my Father, and He solaced me, showed me the path to tread, and made me nobler for the blessedness and pain of that still hour.

Dawn found me an altered man; for in natures like mine the rain of a great sorrow melts the ice of years, and their hidden strength blooms in a late harvest of patience, self−denial, and humility. I resolved to break the tie which bound poor Effie to a joyless fate; and gratitude for a selfish deed, which wore the guise of charity, should no longer mar her peace. I could atone for the wrong I had done her, the suffering she had endured; and she should never know that I had guessed her tender secret, nor learn the love which made my sacrifice so bitter, yet so just.

Alfred came no more; and as I watched the growing pallor of her cheek, her patient efforts to be cheerful and serene, I honored that meek creature for her constance to what she deemed the duty of her life.

I did not tell her my resolve at once, for I could not give her up so soon. It was a weak delay, but I had not learned the beauty of a perfect self−forgetfulness; and though I clung to my purpose steadfastly, my heart still cherished a desperate hope that I might be spared this loss.

In the midst of this secret conflict, there came a letter from old Adam Lyndsay, asking to see his daughter's child; for life was craning slowly, and he desired to forgive, as he hoped to be forgiven then the last hour came. The letter was to me, and, as I read it, I saw

Love and Self Love

a way whereby I might be spared the hard task of telling Effie she was to be free. I feared my near–found strength would desert me, and my courage fail, when, looking on the woman who was dearer to me than my life, I tried to give her back the liberty whose worth she had learned to know.

Effie should go, and I would write the words I dared not speak. She would be in her mother's homes free to show her joy at her release, and smile upon the lover she had banished.

I went to tell her; for it was I who sought her now, who watched for her coming and sighed at her departing steps,— I who waited for her smile and followed her with wistful eyes. The child's slighted affection was atoned for now by my unseen devotion to the woman.

I gave the letter, and she read it silently.

"Will you go, love?" I asked, as she folded it.

" Yes,— the old man has no one to care for him but me, and it is so beautiful to be loved."

A sudden smile touched her lips, and a soft dew shone in the shadowy eyes, which seemed looking into other and tenderer ones than mine. She could not know how sadly I echoed those words, nor how I longed to tell her of another man who sighed to be forgiven.

"You must gather roses for these pale cheeks among the breed moorlands, dear. They are not so blooming as they were a year ago. Jean would reproach me for my want of care," I said, trying to speak cheerfully, though each word seemed a farewell.

"Poor Jean! how long it seems since she kissed them last!" sighed Effie, musing sadly, as she turned her wedding–ring.

My heart ached to see how thin the hand had grown, and how easily that little fetter would fall off when I set my captive lark at liberty.

19

Love and Self Love

I looked till I dared look no longer, and then rose, saying,—

" You will write often, Effie, for I shall miss you very much."

She cast a quick look into my face, asking, hurriedly,—

"Am I to go alone?"

"Dear, I have much to do and cannot go; but you need fear nothing; I shall send Ralph and Mrs. Prior with you, and the journey is soon over. When will you go ? "

It was the first time she had left me since I took her from Jean's arms, and I longed to keep her always near me; but, remembering the task I had to do, I felt that I must seem cold till she knew all.

"Soon,— very soon,— to-morrow,— let me go to-morrow, Sir. I long to be away!" she cried, some swift emotion banishing the calmness of her usual manner, as she rose, with eager eyes and a gesture full of longing.

"You shall go, Effie," was all I could say; and with no word of thanks, she hastened away, leaving me so calm without, so desolate within.

The same eagerness possessed her all that day; and the next she went away, clinging to me at the last as she had clung that night upon the river-bank, as if her grateful heart reproached her for the joy she felt at leaving my unhappy home!

A few days passed, bringing me the comfort of a few sweet lines from Effie signed "Your child." That sight reminded me, that, if I would do an honest deed it should be generously done. I read again the little missive she had sent, and then I wrote the letter which might be my last;— with no hint of my love, beyond the expression of sincerest regard and never-ceasing interest in her happiness; no hint of Alfred Vaughan; for I would not wound her pride, nor let her dream that any eye had seen the passion she so silently surrendered, with no reproach to me and no shadow on the name I had given into her keeping. Heaven knows what it cost me, and Heaven, through the suffering of that hour, granted me an humbler spirit and a better life.

Love and Self Love

It went, and I waited for my fate one might wait for pardon or for doom It came at length,— a short, sad full of meek obedience to my will, of penitence for faults I never knew, and grateful prayers for my peace.

My last hope died then, and for many days I dwelt alone, living over all that happy year with painful vividness. I dreamed again of those fair days, and woke to curse the selfish blindness which had hidden my best blessing from me till it was forever lost.

How long I should have mourned thus unavailingly I cannot tell. A more sudden, but far less grievous loss befell me. My fortune was nearly swept away in the general ruin of a most disastrous year.

This event roused me from my despair and made me strong again,— for I must hoard what could be saved, for Effie's sake. She had known a cruel want with me, and she must never know another while she bore my name. I looked my misfortune in the face and ceased to feel it one; for the diminished fortune was still ample for my darling's dower, and now what need had I of any but the simplest home ?

Before another month was gone, I was in the quiet place henceforth to be mine alone, and nothing now remained for me to do but to dissolve the bond that made Effie mine. Sitting over the dim embers of my solitary hearth, I thought of this, and, looking round the silent room, whose only ornaments were the things made sacred by her use, the utter desolation struck so heavily upon my heart, that I bowed my head upon my folded arms, and yielded to the tender longing that could not be repressed.

The bitter paroxysm passed, and, raising my eyes, the dearer for that stormy rain, I beheld Effie standing like an answer to my spirit's cry.

With a great start, I regarded her, saying, at length, in a voice that sounded cold, for my heart leaped up to meet her, and yet must not speak,—

"Effie, why are you here?"

Wraith–like and pale, she stood before me, with no sign of emotion but the slight tremor of her frame, and answered my greeting with a sad humility:—

Love and Self Love

"I came because I promised to cleave to you through health and sickness, poverty and wealth, and I must keep that vow till you absolve me from it. Forgive me, but I knew misfortune had befallen you, and, remembering all you had done for me, came, hoping I might come when other friends deserted you."

"Grateful to the last! " I sighed, low to myself, and, though deeply touched, replied with the hard−won calmness that made my speech so brief,—

"You owe me nothing, Effie, and I most earnestly desired to spare you this."

Some sudden hope seemed born of my regretful words, for, with an eager glance, she cried,—

" Was it that desire which prompted you to part from me ? Did you think I should shrink from sharing poverty with you who gave me all I own ?"

" No, dear,— ah, no!" I said, "I knew your grateful spirit far too well for that. It was because I could not make your happiness, and yet had robbed you of the right to seek it with some younger and some better man."

"Basil, what man? Tell me; for no doubt shall stand between us now!"

She grasped my arm, and her rapid words were a command.

I only answered, "Alfred Vaughan."

Effie covered up her face, crying, as she sank down at my feet,—

" Oh, my fear! my fear! Why was I blind so long?"

I felt her grief to my heart's core; for my own anguish made me pitiful, and my love made me strong. I lifted up that drooping head and laid it down where it might never rest again, saying, gently, cheerily, and with a most sincere forgetfulness of self,—

"My wife, I never cherished a harsh thought of you, never uttered a reproach when your affections turned from a cold, neglectful guardian, to find a tenderer resting−place. I saw

22

your struggles, dear, your patient grief, your silent sacrifice, and honored you ,more truly than I can tell. Effie, I robbed you of your liberty, but I will restore it, making such poor reparation as I can for this long year of pain; and when I see you blest in a happier home, my keen remorse will be appeased."

As I ceased, Effie rose erect and stood before me, transformed from a timid girl into an earnest woman. Some dormant power and passion woke; she turned on me a countenance aglow with feeling, soul in the eye, heart on the lips, and in her voice an energy that held me mute.

"I feared to speak before," she said "but now I dare anything, for I have heard you call me 'wife,' and seen that in your face which gives me hope. Basil, the grief you saw was not for the loss of any love but yours; the conflict you beheld was the daily struggle to subdue my longing spirit to your will; and the sacrifice you honor but the renunciation of all hope. I stood between you and the woman whom you loved, and asked of death to free me frown that cruel lot. You gave me back my life, but you withhold the gift that made it worth possessing. You desired to be freed from the affection which only wearied you, and I tried to conquer it; but it would not die. Let me speak now, and then I will be still forever! Must our ways lie apart? Can I never be more to you than now? Oh, Basil! oh, my husband! I have loved you very truly from the first! Shall I never know the blessedness of a return?"

Words could not answer that appeal. I gathered my life's happiness close to my breast, and in the silence of a full heart felt that God was very good to me.

Soon all my pain and passion were confessed. Fast and fervently the tale was told; and as the truth dawned on that patient wife, a tender peace transfigured her uplifted countenance, until to me it seemed an angel's face.

"I am a poor man now," I said, still holding that frail creature fast, fearing to see her vanish, as her semblance had so often done in the long vigils I had kept,— "a poor man, Effie, and yet very rich, for I have my treasure back again. But I am wiser than when we parted; for I have learned that love is better than a world of wealth, and victory over self a nobler conquest than a continent. Dear, I have no home but this. Can you be happy here, with no fortune but the little store set apart for you, and the knowledge that no want shall touch you while I live?"

Love and Self Love

And as I spoke, I sighed, remembering all I might have done, and dreading poverty for her alone.

But with a gesture, soft, yet solemn, Effie laid her hands upon my head, as if endowing me with blessing and with gift, and answered, with her steadfast eyes on mine,—

"You gave me your home when I was homeless; let me give it back, and with it a proud wife. I, too, am rich; for that old man is gone and left me all. Take it, Basil, and give me a little love."

I gave not little, but a long life of devotion for the good gift God had bestowed on me,— finding in it a household spirit the daily benediction of whose presence banished sorrow, selfishness, and gloom, and, through the influence of happy human love, led me to a truer faith in the Divine.

CPSIA information can be obtained
at www.ICGtesting.com
Printed in the USA
BVHW070721220620
581990BV00003B/308

9 781162 671871